D1609189

THE PUSH
FOR **SOCIAL**
CHANGE

The Women's Rights Movement

Don Nardo

ReferencePoint
Press®

San Diego, CA

About the Author

Historian and award-winning writer Don Nardo has written many books for young people about American history, including The Salem Witch Trials, The American Revolution, The Mexican-American War, The Declaration of Independence, The Great Depression, and biographies of Thomas Jefferson, Andrew Johnson, Franklin D. Roosevelt, and Barack Obama. Mr. Nardo, who also composes orchestral music, lives with his wife, Christine, in Massachusetts.

© 2019 ReferencePoint Press, Inc.
Printed in the United States

For more information, contact:
ReferencePoint Press, Inc.
PO Box 27779
San Diego, CA 92198
www.ReferencePointPress.com

3 4873 00544 1928

LIBRARY OF CONGRESS CATALOGING-IN-PUBLICATION DATA

Name: Nardo, Don, 1947– author.
Title: The Women's Rights Movement/by Don Nardo.
Description: San Diego, CA: ReferencePoint Press, [2018] | Series: The Push for Social Change | Audience: Grade 9 to 12. | Includes bibliographical references and index.
Identifiers: LCCN 2018001350 (print) | LCCN 2018002714 (ebook) | ISBN 9781682824269 (eBook) | ISBN 9781682824252 (hardback)
Subjects: LCSH: Women's rights—United States—History—Juvenile literature. | Feminism—History—Juvenile literature.
Classification: LCC HQ1236.5.U6 (ebook) | LCC HQ1236.5.U6 N367 2018 (print) | DDC 305.420973—dc23
LC record available at https://lccn.loc.gov/2018001350

CONTENTS

IMPORTANT EVENTS IN THE WOMEN'S RIGHTS MOVEMENT

1848
Lucretia Mott and Elizabeth Cady Stanton cohost the first women's rights convention in Seneca Falls, New York.

1920
The law passed by Congress allowing women to vote is ratified by a majority of the states and goes into effect.

1650
Anne Bradstreet of the Massachusetts Bay Colony releases her first book of poetry, becoming the first woman to be published in the American colonies.

1890
The American Woman Suffrage Association and another major women's group combine, forming the National American Woman Suffrage Association.

1650 /	1830	1860	1890	1920

1821
Vermont native Emma Willard opens the first private girl's high school in Troy, New York.

1911
One hundred and forty-six people, mostly women, die in the Triangle Shirtwaist Company fire in New York City.

1862
Nurse Clara Barton distinguishes both herself and her gender by saving lives while under enemy fire during the Civil War's Battle of Antietam.

1918
The US Congress passes legislation allowing for women's suffrage.

1869
Lucy Stone and some colleagues establish the American Woman Suffrage Association with the goal of bringing about female voting rights.

1982
Having passed Congress several years before, the Equal Rights Amendment is not ratified by the number of states needed to become law.

2017
Hundreds of American women accuse male public figures of sexually harassing them, launching the enormous #MeToo social movement.

1972
Women's rights activist Gloria Steinem founds *Ms.*, a magazine dedicated to women and their social problems and aspirations.

1933
President Franklin D. Roosevelt appoints Frances Perkins secretary of labor, making her the first woman to serve in a US presidential cabinet.

2009
President Barack Obama signs into law the Lilly Ledbetter Fair Pay Act.

1930   **1950**   **1970**   **1990**   **2010**

1932
Arkansas's Hattie Caraway becomes the first woman to be elected to the US Senate.

1960
About 39 percent of American women work outside the home.

1992
In this so-called Year of the Woman, twenty-four women win seats in the House of Representatives and three women win seats in the Senate.

2018
For the second year in a row, hundreds of thousands of women march nationwide to protest government policies on a variety of issues; marchers focus on women's rights, human rights, and encouraging women to vote and run for office.

1963
President John F. Kennedy signs into law the Equal Pay Act, which helps women begin to close the wage inequality gap with men.

1941
With the US entry into World War II, some 18 million women take jobs outside the home in support of the war effort.

American Suffragists and the Night of Terror

For most young Americans growing up today, it is hard to imagine that less than a century ago women had far fewer rights than they do now. Indeed, for the first 144 years of the nation's existence, they were not even allowed to vote. Eventually women started to protest this gross inequity and to lobby for their right to use the ballot box. The protesters, known as suffragists (because *suffrage* means the right to vote), wrote newspaper articles, marched in parades, and picketed government offices to further their cause.

One Inhumane Act After Another

During the summer of 1917, for example, large numbers of suffragists picketed the White House. Their goal was to convince President Woodrow Wilson, who had long largely ignored the protests, to support the cause of women's suffrage. Initially, the Washington, DC, police left the picketers alone, reasoning that trying to stop them would only provide them with the publicity they desired.

In time, however, the local authorities decided it was time to act, and they ordered their officers to begin arresting the protesters. The hope was that if the picketers spent a day or two in jail they would be discouraged enough to quit protesting. But to the surprise of the police, after serving their short sentences, all of the arrested women went right back to picketing the White House.

Frustrated, the police tried a different, more aggressive approach—to make an example of the protesters' leader, Alice Paul. An outspoken, no-nonsense kind of person, she carried a banner that bore the words that President Wilson had recently used in connection with the US entry into World War I: "The time has come to conquer or submit, for us there can be but one choice. We have made it."[1] The fact that those words could also be applied to the suffragists and their quest for justice greatly annoyed the male police authorities. Feeling that Paul's audacity gave them an excuse to teach her a lesson, they arrested her on October 20, 1917.

At the urging of the police, a local judge immediately sentenced Paul to seven months in prison. Undaunted, within days of entering the jail she boldly staged a hunger strike. She later recalled, "It was the strongest weapon left with which to continue [our] battle."[2] Indeed, as she likely expected would happen, other imprisoned suffragists were inspired by her example and also refused to eat.

This display of bravery not only surprised and embarrassed police officials, but it also made them indignant and angry. Bent on retaliation, they tried to persecute Paul by placing her in a ward for psychopathic, or insane, inmates. When her rebellious attitude remained intact, they put bright lights in her cell to prevent her from sleeping. The intrepid Paul still refused to yield and continued her hunger strike. Hearing this, the warden, W.H. Whittaker, had the guards hold her down, brutally push a tube down her throat, and force liquids into her stomach. This torture went on several times a day for weeks.

Despite this savage mistreatment, Paul valiantly refused to cooperate or admit defeat. A doctor examined her during her torment and told the warden and some other officials that they were wasting their time. She possessed "a spirit like Joan of Arc," he told them, "and it is useless to try to change it. She will die but she will never give up."[3] Meanwhile, a number of the other imprisoned women suffered the same ordeal of cruel force-feeding. Also, the cornmeal and beans that other inmates ate for their regular meals contained worms and other parasites. One plucky woman put some of the worms on a spoon and told a guard to take it to Warden Whittaker. Needless to say, the gesture only made him even angrier with the suffragists.

> "She will die but she will never give up."[3]
>
> —A prison doctor describing suffragist leader Alice Paul

A group of suffragists protest the imprisonment of their leader, Alice Paul, who was given a particularly harsh sentence of seven months in jail for demanding the right to vote.

WE DEMAND
THAT THE
AMERICAN GOVERNMENT GIVE
ALICE PAUL
A POLITICAL OFFENDER,
THE PRIVILEGES RUSSIA GAVE MIYUNOFF

TO ASK FREEDOM
FOR WOMEN IS NOT
A CRIME
SUFFRAGE PRISONERS
SHOULD NOT BE TREATED
AS CRIMINALS

A Scene of Havoc

When Whittaker and other police authorities saw that their bullying tactics were not working, they resorted to overt violence. One of the most shameful episodes in American history took place in that Washington, DC, jail during the evening of November 15, 1917. Later, historians came to call it the Night of Terror.

After sundown, Whittaker gathered between forty and fifty burly guards, some borrowed from a local men's prison, and entered the cell block housing the suffragists. At the warden's order, the small army of guards, who were armed with clubs, attacked the women. They pounded them with the clubs and also kicked, slapped, and choked them. One of the victims later recalled,

> The guards brought from the male prison fell upon us. I saw Miss Lincoln, a slight young girl, thrown to the floor. Mrs. Nolan, a delicate old lady of seventy-three, was [roughed up] by two men. The furniture was overturned, and the room

was a scene of havoc. Whittaker, [standing] in the center of the room, directed the whole attack, inciting the guards to every brutality. The whole group of women were thrown, dragged, and hurled [about].[4]

Washington Post reporter Terence McArdle adds, "The guards threw suffragist Dora Lewis into a dark cell and smashed her head against an iron bed, knocking her out. Lewis's cellmate, Alice Cosu, believing Lewis dead, suffered a heart attack and was denied medical care until the next morning."[5]

The Battle Goes On

This brazen, barbaric effort to terrorize the suffragists and make them give up their quest for voting rights failed miserably. Newspapers across the nation swiftly learned of the events in the jail, and most of the US public was shocked. Hearing about the brutalities the jailed women had endured, large numbers of Americans who had formerly expressed doubts about women's suffrage changed their minds. One of these former skeptics was President Wilson.

With his support, less than three years later, in 1920, the US Constitution was amended, and American women voted for the first time.

Led by strong, fearless individuals like Paul, American women had triumphed in the face of adversity and overcome a daunting challenge. Paul, who lived until 1977, recognized that women faced many other hurdles.

> "[The warden] directed the whole attack, inciting the guards to every brutality."[4]
>
> —An imprisoned suffragist's memory of the Night of Terror

As the modern institute named for her says, "Her life symbolizes the long struggle for justice in the United States and around the world. Her vision was the ordinary notion that women and men should be equal partners in society."[6] As late as 2018, that state of total equality still had not been achieved. So the battle begun by Paul and other gallant leaders of the American women's rights movement continues today.

CHAPTER ONE

Centuries of Second-Class Citizenship

American anthropologist Margaret Mead, who died in 1978, famously said, "Never doubt that a small group of thoughtful, committed citizens can change the world. Indeed, it's the only thing that ever has."[7] Mead's reference was to various groups around the globe and throughout history. Yet her words have often been applied to the American women's rights movement.

The year 2018 marked the 170th anniversary of that movement's launching. In 1848 a small group of women met in upstate New York to address the issue of women's equality in America. The ultimate fruits of their efforts, members of the National Women's History Project point out, have been truly staggering changes for women, including

> in family life, in religion, in government, in employment, in education. These changes did not just happen spontaneously. Women themselves made these changes happen, very deliberately. Women have not been the passive recipients of miraculous changes in laws and human nature. [Several] generations of women have come together to effect these changes in the most democratic ways: through meetings, petition drives, lobbying, public speaking, and nonviolent resistance. They have worked very deliberately to create a better world, and they have succeeded hugely.[8]

Were Women Naturally Subservient?

The major inequalities between men and women in American society, which the women's rights movement began to address during the 1840s, were an integral facet of everyday life and had been since the very founding of colonial America during the 1600s. Legally, socially, and politically, the earliest American women were decidedly second-class citizens. A woman's social class did play a role—upper-class women were seen as socially superior to both women and men of the lower classes. Yet regardless of class, no woman could vote or hold political office.

> "Never doubt that a small group of thoughtful, committed citizens can change the world."[7]
> —American anthropologist Margaret Mead

Overall, colonial American women had almost no civil (or civic) rights, a situation that was destined to prevail throughout the colonial period and well beyond.

Colonial men, of course, took it for granted that this unequal status quo was the natural order of things, ordained by God and the church. As a result, they were not hesitant to publicly state their attitude regarding women and gender roles. One of the more memorable of these statements was made during the 1630s by John Winthrop, who served as governor of the Massachusetts Bay Colony. In any marriage, he said, the husband is the wife's lord and she must follow his rules and orders to the letter. She could think of herself as "safe and free," he said, only if she fully accepted "her subjection to her husband's authority." Further, this was the social reality that Jesus Christ, the English king, and her husband all agreed was best. The husband's control over her "is so easy and sweet to her as a bride's ornaments. And if, through forwardness and wantonness [impulsiveness], etc., she shakes [that control] off at any time, she is at no rest in her spirit until she takes it up again. And whether her lord smiles upon her and embraces her in his arms, or rebukes [scolds] or smites [hits] her, she apprehends the sweetness of his love."[9]

Thanks to the overwhelming control exerted by men over women in colonial America's early period, women had virtually no legal rights. A married woman was not allowed to keep or spend her own wages, even if she had a job, which was very uncommon; she could not sign a contract; she could not sell a piece of property, even if she had inherited it; nor could she have custody of her children if she was separated from her husband. Moreover, if she desired a divorce, she could legally obtain one only if her husband regularly beat her brutally or deserted her.

To explain why this state of affairs was perfectly acceptable, many men fell back on the theory that God created women specifically to be subservient to men. Among the Puritans of Massachusetts, for example, the belief was that whereas men were

In early American settlements such as the Massachusetts Bay Colony, women were second-class citizens, a status that men assumed was ordained by God and the church.

naturally morally superior beings, women were inherently weaker and less moral because of the sins committed by the world's first woman. This idea was "based on scriptural texts that reflect the male-centered worldview of the times in which they were written," says Harvard divinity professor Catherine A. Brekus. "Based on the account in [the Bible], many [colonial Christians] argued that Eve's decision to eat the forbidden fruit in the Garden of Eden brought sin and suffering into the world. According to this interpretation, God ordained women to submit to the authority of their fathers and husbands because of Eve's disobedience."[10]

Hard Labor and a Lack of Education

Partly because colonial women were viewed as morally inferior second-class citizens, they often bore the brunt of much of the menial toil required to keep the colonies functioning. According to one authority on colonial American life, a housewife during the 1600s and 1700s performed long hours of backbreaking labor daily: "In a frontier settlement, housekeeping was only part of her duties. She helped to clear the land and build the house and plant the crops as well. Even when she lived in a village of snug, comfortable houses, her daily tasks filled every hour from sunrise to long after sunset."[11]

Building and maintaining houses and planting crops occupied only some of those long, grinding hours for colonial wives. They also were society's child bearers. Whether they liked it or not, they had to carry and give birth to children, which quite often numbered eight or ten, and families with fourteen or more children were not uncommon.

Infant and child mortality was prevalent in the colonies. The causes of disease were unknown, and medicine was archaic compared to its modern state. At least four out of every ten children born in that society were dead by age six. Hence, for its survival society pushed women into having large numbers of babies, which took a heavy toll on the health of many mothers. (Lack of effective methods of birth control was also a factor in the large size of families.) Moreover, the children that lived and prospered

Haunting Refrains

Anne Bradstreet (1612–1672) of the Massachusetts Bay Colony was the first colonial American woman to have her works published. Her first volume of poetry, which appeared in 1650, received positive reviews both in America and Europe. The lovely, to some degree haunting, sentiments in the following excerpt (from "Before the Birth of One of Her Children") is typical of her work.

All things within this fading world have end,
Adversity does still our joys attend;
No ties so strong, no friends so dear and sweet,
But with deaths parting blow is sure to meet.
The sentence past is most irrevocable [final],
A common thing, yet oh inevitable;
How soon, my Dear, death may my steps attend,
How soon it may be your lot to lose your friend,
We both are ignorant, yet love bids me
These farewell lines to recommend to thee,
That when that knot's untied that made us one,
I may seem yours, who in effect am none.
And if I see not half my day's that's due,
What nature would, God grant to yours and you.

Quoted in Anne Bradstreet, "Before the Birth of One of Her Children," Early Americas Digital Archive. http://eada .lib.umd.edu.

had to be fed, cared for, clothed, watched, and disciplined. All of these child care duties fell to women.

Escaping this relentless grind of work and responsibility was extremely difficult for women. For men, getting some sort of education was one way to improve one's life situation, but at first almost no educational opportunities existed for colonial women. One minor exception was among the Puritans of Massachusetts Bay. They strongly emphasized learning, and a few women in the colony were allowed to learn to read and write. Anne Bradstreet was one, and she became the first female American to publish a piece of literature. A small section of one of her many poems, "Four Ages of Man," reads,

I've seen unworthy men advanced high,
(And better ones suffer extremity)
But neither favor, riches, title, State,
Could length their days or once reverse their fate
I've seen one stabbed, and some to lose their heads
And others fly, struck both with guilt and dread.
I've seen and so have you, for tis but late,
The desolation of a goodly State.[12]

In the American colonies, Bradstreet's education and literary output remained a rarity. Most American women of the 1600s and even the 1700s could neither read nor write. A few did learn these skills through parental instruction in the home. But overall women lacked formal education partly because a majority of men accepted the beliefs of male philosophers such as eighteenth-century Swiss theorist Jean-Jacques Rousseau. A woman's main role in life, he said, was to support and please a man.

Clearly, almost all colonial women during Rousseau's era lacked the education and opportunities to refute literary giants of his stature. It was not until 1818, therefore, that a female essayist hailing from Boston—Hannah Mather Crocker—presented a proper rebuttal to Rousseau. In her book *Observations on the Real Rights of Women*, she points out that "there can be no doubt" that if women "received the same mode of education [as men do], their [personal and social] improvement would be fully equal."[13]

> "[If women] received the same mode of education [as men do], their [personal and social] improvement would be fully equal."[13]
>
> —Nineteenth-century female essayist Hannah Mather Crocker

Female High Schools and Colleges

In the late 1700s a handful of American towns, mostly in New England, began funding elementary education for young girls. But such classes were few in number, privately run, and did not teach the girls much beyond basic literacy skills. It was during Crocker's lifetime that the notion of educating larger numbers of women and teaching them more than just reading and writing began to gain some traction. In 1819 New York governor Dewitt Clinton backed an educational project suggested to him by Vermont native Emma Willard—a secondary school (today called a high school) for teenage girls. The school opened in Troy, New York, in 1821. The girls took courses in geography, history, and science, the same subjects offered in secondary schools for boys.

One drawback of Willard's school was that it was private and catered solely to the daughters of well-to-do parents. The first public school for girls, which admitted students of varied means, opened in 1824 in Worcester, Massachusetts. After that, a movement to build more public schools for young women steadily gained momentum. Spearheading this effort were members of a new generation of bold female writers, prominent among them Scottish-born Frances Wright. She believed that the only way women could achieve any sort of equality with men was for both genders to receive comparable educations.

At the same time that the barriers against high schools for young women were beginning to erode, a few female rights advocates dared to propose the then-radical idea of women attending college. Oberlin College, established in Ohio in 1833, began admitting women later in that decade. One of the school's first female graduates, Antoinette Brown, went on to become America's first female ordained minister.

During these same years another women's rights activist, Catharine Beecher, gained prominence. She pointed out women's substandard opportunities for decent jobs. Many young women, she said, toiled in eastern manufacturing towns like Lowell, Massachusetts, where, by the 1850s, thousands of women worked long hours in textile mills for very little pay. Beecher held that it would be more productive for more young women to become teachers. Teaching was a safer, more dignified profession, she argued. Her promotion of this concept became the basis for a chain of so-called normal schools, which were colleges designed to

A woman operates a loom in an early 20th century textile mill. Starting in the 1850s, women's rights activist Catharine Beecher argued that women should train to become teachers rather than work in textile mills.

train teachers. To drum up support for the plan, in 1852 Beecher established the American Women's Educational Association.

The advent of the teacher training that Beecher championed had enormous consequences. For the first time, large numbers of American women were able to find employment outside their homes that required them to use their minds and talents rather than do unremitting, backbreaking physical labor. A major barrier to female social equality in the United States had been shattered.

From Abolitionism to Women's Rights

During the period of the 1830s and 1840s, as American women's educational opportunities began to significantly expand, their long movement toward equality gained another boost that came from an unexpected quarter. It was abolitionism, the struggle to abolish slavery. In the three decades preceding the American Civil War (1861–1865), slavery became an increasingly controversial issue in the country. As the abolitionist movement expanded, it attracted large numbers of women. They recognized a strong similarity

A Woman Ahead of Her Time

Frances Wright (1795–1852) is now a largely forgotten heroine of the early women's rights movement. One reason why her name is not invoked very often is because her views were extremely liberal for her day. During the 1820s, for instance, she established a racially mixed community of abolitionists in Nashobe, Tennessee, and there advocated intermarriage of whites and blacks, for which society condemned her as immoral. She was also severely criticized for calling on men to be more understanding of women's plight as second-class citizens. In one of her many public lectures on social justice, she called out to fathers and husbands, saying,

> Do ye not see how, in the mental bondage of your wives and fair companions, you yourselves are bound? Will you fondly sport yourselves in your imagined liberty, and say, "it matters not if our women be mental slaves?" Will you pleasure yourselves in the varied paths of knowledge, and imagine that women, hoodwinked and unawakened, will make the better servants and the easier playthings? They are greatly in error who [are trapped in that sexist mind-set], as many a bankrupt merchant and sinking mechanic, not to say drowning capitalists, could bear witness. But setting aside dollars and cents, which men, in their present uncomfortable state of existence, are but too prone exclusively to regard, how many nobler interests of the mind and the heart cry "treason!" to this false calculation [about women]?

Frances Wright, *Course of Popular Lectures: With Three Addresses, on Various Public Occasions, and a Reply to the Charges Against the French Reformers of 1789.* London: James Watson, 1834, pp. 20–21.

between racial equality and gender equality, so it seemed only natural for them to come to the aid of slaves, who formed another group of people dominated by white men.

Female activists also learned a lot of practical lessons from working in the abolitionist movement. According to scholar Faye E. Dudden,

> Abolitionism provided women with sympathetic male allies [who] took them seriously and publicized their cause, while the "school of anti-slavery" gave them practical experience with agitation through passing petitions, circulating pamphlets, sending out itinerant speakers, and calling "conventions." Just as important, abolition trained its

adherents to withstand ridicule and hostility; as extreme radicals, they had already seen social [condemnation] and even mob violence. Because of its abolitionist roots, this early women's rights movement was confined wholly to the northern states, and slaveholding southerners mocked women's rights as a symptom of northern degeneracy.[14]

Among the leading female abolitionists was Lucretia Coffin Mott. She and her husband, James, along with other antislavery activists, including sisters Sarah and Angelina Grimké, tirelessly traveled through northern states. In their numerous public speeches, they denounced slavery and linked the issues of slaves' freedom and women's equality. Also hugely influential in the movement was Harriet Beecher Stowe, the daughter of a northern minister and the half sister of Catharine Beecher. Her 1852 book *Uncle Tom's Cabin*—about a slave who is beaten to death by his vicious master—became a best seller and convinced numerous women and men to become abolitionists.

Not long before Stowe's book was published, two prominent female abolitionists decided that they simply could not wait for the end of slavery to begin fighting specifically for women's rights. They were Lucretia Mott and her close friend Elizabeth Cady Stanton, who lived in Seneca Falls, a small town in upstate New York. The two had initially met at the World Anti-Slavery Convention in London in 1840. During the years that followed, they periodically talked about organizing to expand women's rights. But it was not until the summer of 1848 that they felt they were ready to begin.

> "Slaveholding southerners mocked women's rights as a symptom of northern degeneracy."[14]
>
> —Scholar Faye E. Dudden

As a first step, Mott, Stanton, and some other women's rights activists placed an ad in the July 4 issue of the *Seneca County Courier*. It read, in part, "Women's Rights Convention—A convention to discuss the social, civil, and religious rights of women, will be held in the Wesleyan Chapel, Seneca Falls, New York, on

THE FIRST CONVENTION

EVER CALLED TO DISCUSS THE

Civil and Political Rights of Women,

SENECA FALLS, N. Y., JULY 19, 20, 1848.

————

WOMAN'S RIGHTS CONVENTION.

————

A Convention to discuss the social, civil, and religious condition and rights of woman will be held in the Wesleyan Chapel, at Seneca Falls, N. Y., on Wednesday and Thursday, the 19th and 20th of July current; commencing at 10 o'clock A. M. During the first day the meeting will be exclusively for women, who are earnestly invited to attend. The public generally are invited to be present on the second day, when Lucretia Mott, of Philadelphia, and other ladies and gentlemen, will address the Convention.*

Two prominent activists, Elizabeth Cady Stanton and Lucretia Mott, placed an advertisement in the *Seneca County Courier*, inviting women to attend a convention in Seneca Falls, New York, in July 1848.

Wednesday and Thursday, the 19th and 20th of July. . . . During the first day the meeting will be held exclusively for women."[15]

"Woman Stands by the Side of Man"

The historic meeting proved an unqualified success. To Mott and Stanton's surprise, forty men showed up on the first day, even though the ad had stipulated it would be for women only. Among these male attendees was the great African American thinker, author, and activist Frederick Douglass. The organizers happily seated the men along with the roughly 240 women who attended.

The two days were filled with lively discussions and speeches. One of the keynote addresses was delivered by Stanton herself, who said, in part,

[A] woman alone can understand the height, the depth, the length, and breadth of her degradation and woe. Man cannot speak for us—because he has been educated to believe that we differ from him so materially, that he cannot judge of our thoughts, feelings, and opinions by his own. [We here today] dare assert that woman stands by the side of man—his equal, placed here by her God, to enjoy with him the beautiful earth.[16]

Stanton also composed a document called the "Declaration of Sentiments and Resolutions." Constructed in the same style as the US Declaration of Independence, it listed several of the ways that men had created a system rigged for men and against women. Women could not vote, for instance, which meant that they had to obey laws they had no say in making. Inequities in divorce, property rights, and numerous other social and legal areas were also addressed.

The Seneca Falls Convention, as it came to be called, turned out to have profound effects that even its organizers did not completely foresee. Not surprisingly, the male-controlled press criticized and mocked the meeting afterward. Although this dismayed Mott and Stanton, they reasoned that at least they had gotten the word out that American women needed to organize for their rights. Stanton told people, "It will start women thinking, and men too; and when men and women think about a new question, the first step in progress is taken."[17]

In retrospect, she was being naively modest. The Seneca Falls meeting later came to be seen as the official beginning of both the fight for female suffrage and the larger US women's rights movement. Moreover, for their roles in organizing it, in the fullness of time Stanton and Mott became nothing less than human rights immortals.

CHAPTER TWO

Women Learn to Fight for Their Rights

Although the 1848 Seneca Falls Convention represented the official initiation of a formal women's rights movement in the United States, its beneficial effects for women were far from immediate. Indeed, of the more than 240 women who attended the meeting, only one—Charlotte Woodward—was destined to live long enough to actually vote in an election. The fact that it would be a long time before American women were taken seriously in the political sphere was well illustrated by male reactions to the Seneca Falls meeting. Newspapers and journals—all controlled by men—dismissed the gathering and its leaders.

For example, the *Oneida Whig*, the principal newspaper in nearby Oneida, New York, said of the convention, "Was there ever such a dreadful revolt?" The meeting was a would-be rebellion, the editors said. It was "the most shocking and unnatural incident ever recorded in the history of womanity," they asserted. "If our ladies will insist on voting and legislating, where, gentlemen, will be our dinners? . . . [And who will mend] the holes in our stockings?"[18] Another Upstate New York paper, Albany's *Mechanic's Advocate*, similarly ridiculed the Seneca Falls gathering. "It requires no argument to prove that this is all wrong," an editor lectured. "Every true hearted female will instantly feel that this is unwomanly."[19]

Unflattering Male Reactions

One thing these male editors did not expect was that their open disrespect for women would backfire. Unwittingly, such media mockery gave the convention's organizers a lot of free publicity.

Historians Bonnie Eisenberg and Mary Ruthsdotter point out that "people in cities and isolated towns alike were now alerted to the issues, and joined this heated discussion of women's rights in great numbers!"[20]

Indeed, Mott, Stanton, and their colleagues had hoped that their gathering might spur enough interest to inspire other similar female conventions, and that wish was soon fulfilled. The second women's convention took place in 1850 in Worcester, Massachusetts. Between 1850 and 1860 the trend continued, with national women's rights conventions being held every year, except in 1857. Moreover, during each of those years many smaller women's gatherings were held in most northern states.

> "If our ladies will insist on voting and legislating, where, gentlemen, will be our dinners?"[18]
>
> —An editor at the *Oneida Whig* on the 1848 Seneca Falls Convention

The reactions of the male-dominated press to these meetings continued to be predictable. One editor demanded to know what the organizers of the gatherings could possibly want. After all, he said, surely they must realize that women would never achieve the same rights as men. Typical was an editorial in a New York City newspaper in 1853, which stated that the conventions' attendees had stepped "out of their appropriate sphere"—that is, the home. They sought to "mingle in the busy walks of everyday life." In so doing they were neglecting "those duties which both human and divine law have assigned to them." The editor conveniently failed to mention that by that time more than a quarter of women in the northern states worked either part or full time in factories, clearly outside the "sphere" of the home. His omission likely stemmed from his reluctance to encourage a trend he did not want to see continue. Indeed, he did his best to discourage women from seeking equality, even going so far as to criticize the women's rights organizers on their looks. They "are entirely devoid of personal attractions," he railed. "They are generally thin maiden ladies [who] violate the rules of decency and taste by attiring themselves in eccentric [clothes], which hang loosely and inelegantly upon their forms, making [them] an object of aversion and disgust."[21]

Rising to War's Challenge

After more than a decade in which women's rights activists had persevered despite such small-minded criticisms, in 1861 the forward momentum of the women's rights movement suddenly slowed. This was the year that the United States plunged into the bloody Civil War. Some female activists felt that the conflict should not deter them. They wanted to forge ahead with demands for their rights even as the country was torn asunder.

A majority of women, however, rejected that strategy. Whether residing in the North or the South, they felt that aiding their fathers and husbands in the war effort must take precedence over personal political issues. The famous author of *Little Women*, Louisa May Alcott, summed up the attitude of most American women when she said, "I long to be a man. But as I can't fight, I will content myself with working for those who can."[22]

Hundreds of thousands of American women acted on these words in one way or another during the war years. Rising to the challenge, some operated family farms and businesses while their husbands or fathers were away serving in the military. Others served as postal workers, office clerks, secretaries, nurses, and seamstresses who sewed uniforms, to name only a few of the jobs that women took on.

The women who became nurses were especially prominent in the conflict. More than three thousand of the North's nurses during the war were women, although they were still outnumbered by the male nurses, who were typically assigned to the front lines. The female nurses toiled diligently in both traditional hospitals and makeshift clinics set up near the battlefronts. The most renowned of these women was a Massachusetts native named Clara Barton. In the midst of the bloody Battle of Antietam in September 1862, she assumed a role usually taken by male nurses by driving a wagon loaded with medical supplies

> "[Clara Barton is] the true hero of the age, the angel of the battlefield."[23]
>
> —Union doctor James Dunn

Women in Brooklyn meet to organize a fair meant to raise money and provide supplies for soldiers in the Civil War. A majority of women, both Northern and Southern, gave priority to supporting troops instead of advocating for women's rights.

and food right onto the battlefield. As bullets whizzed around her, including one that penetrated one of her sleeves, she spent many hours tending to the needs of hundreds of wounded men. The doctor in charge of her unit, James Dunn, was astounded at her courage and dedication to duty. He later called her "the true hero of the age, the angel of the battlefield."[23]

Postwar Disappointment

The efforts of Barton and thousands of other enterprising women during the war had a major bearing on the future of the women's rights movement. Many men who had previously considered women to be their inferiors were hugely impressed and came to see the female sex in a different light. Likely no one summarized this altered perception of women better than President Abraham Lincoln. "If all that has been said by orators and poets since the creation of the world were applied to the women of America," he stated, "it would not do them justice for their conduct during the war."[24]

Nevertheless, although the efforts of many women during the war had enhanced their general image, most men holding the reins of power were not yet ready to grant women equality. The idea of female suffrage, for instance, remained unpopular among most men. Nor were male bosses ready to pay female workers the same wages they paid male workers. It was therefore clear to the leaders of the women's rights movement that their struggle for equality would be long and hard.

Underscoring this sad fact was an overpowering sense of disappointment among many women for the way Congress amended the US Constitution in the years immediately following the war. All Americans expected lawmakers to make the Constitution reflect the fact that slavery was abolished. The two amendments in question—the fourteenth and fifteenth since the nation's founding—would grant African Americans citizenship and the right to vote. Female activists saw the legislation as a golden opportunity to give voting rights to women—both white and black—as well as to black men.

Yet when the amendments were ratified in 1868 and 1870 respectively, they gave African American men suffrage, but not women. A disillusioned Stanton remarked that the new laws "would allow men to continue dominating women."[25] She added, "There is no patriotism, no true nobility in tamely and silently submitting to this insult." The amendments, she said, endorsed "the old idea that women's divinely ordained position is at men's feet, and not on an even platform by his side."[26]

Stanton and some other women in the movement were so upset that they started suggesting that white women deserved the right to vote more than black men. However, a number of other female activists felt that this racially charged attitude was both unfair and unbecoming. As a result, Lucy Stone and a group of activists established a new organization, the American Woman Suffrage Association, in 1869. In response, Stanton and her colleague Susan B. Anthony formed a rival group, the National Women's Suffrage Association.

Striving for Better Working Conditions

While these organizations concentrated primarily on attaining the right to vote, other female activists concentrated their energies on bettering women's working conditions. Working women were nothing new in the United States both before and after the Civil War. In 1860, on the eve of the conflict, some sixty-two thousand women worked in New England textile mills alone. In fact, in that same year almost 30 percent of all workers in US manufacturing were women.

A primary reason why factory owners employed so many women was because they traditionally earned considerably less than men for the same job. For example, in a job that paid a man $.75 a day, a woman was paid $.25, and if a woman made $.50

Poor Planning Leads to Disaster

The deaths of so many women workers in the infamous 1911 Triangle Factory fire was preventable. After the disaster, police and fire inspectors found that poor planning and other mistakes by the owners were to blame. First, the company had never staged any fire drills. That precaution was badly needed in a workplace in which several different languages were spoken and escape instructions in English during a fire would be confusing to the women who understood little English.

The main reason so many women workers on the ninth floor perished, however, was that they were locked in. The company's owners had recently instituted a policy designed to stop employees on that floor from stealing cloth and tools when leaving work. Under that policy, all of the ninth-floor exits were locked and the owners opened one at the end of the workday. At that exit, guards checked the employees' bags for possible stolen items. Thus, with all their exits blocked, the workers on the ninth floor were trapped as the flames roared through the building's upper stories. In contrast, the workers on the tenth floor had access to the stairs. By climbing them, they were able to reach the roof, where workers in nearby taller buildings lowered ladders to them so they could escape.

per day to do some form of work, a man received about $1.50 for the same work. Thus, a business owner who hired mostly women made higher profits.

In addition to paying women less, business owners exploited them in other ways. Typically, a female worker enjoyed no chance of promotion to a less menial, higher-paying position. Also, if a woman made some sort of mistake on the job, the boss often docked her pay. Furthermore, women were frequently forced to work sixty, seventy, or even eighty hours per week, and their working conditions were often substandard and/or physically dangerous. In 1860, for instance, the roof of a textile mill in Lawrence, Massachusetts, collapsed onto the workers, killing more than a hundred people, most of them women.

In hopes of rectifying these working conditions, during the middle to late 1800s female workers sometimes went on strike. The problem was that this tactic almost always failed. Often the owner of the affected business simply fired the strike's organizers and threatened to terminate the other strikers if they did not return to work at the same level of pay as before.

Nevertheless, in each new generation increasing numbers of dedicated female activists strove to better organize women and train them to fight for workplace reforms. Elizabeth Gurley Flynn was one of those activists. She wrote a number of pamphlets and articles urging women to advocate for improved workplace conditions. In one, she said, "Women are in industry to stay. They cannot be driven back to the home. [They] are part of the army of labor and must be organized and disciplined as such, [because when] organized they are tenacious and true fighters."[27]

> "[When] organized they are tenacious and true fighters."[27]
>
> —Female activist Elizabeth Gurley Flynn on working women

As time went on, the efforts of labor organizers like Flynn did effect some minimal changes that were beneficial for women in certain areas and cities. But overall it turned out that a large proportion of the workplace reforms that women finally obtained came from public outrage over disasters like the Lawrence roof collapse. Most

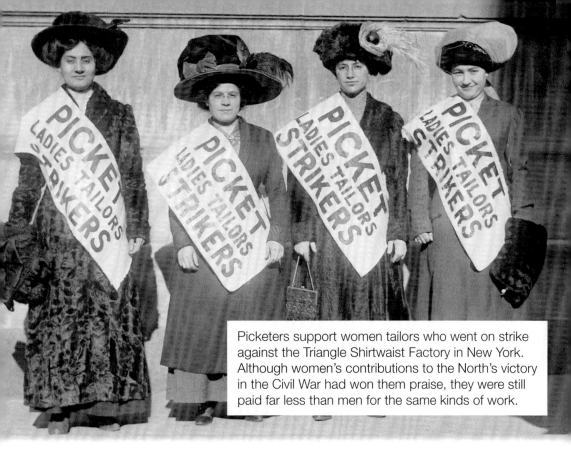

Picketers support women tailors who went on strike against the Triangle Shirtwaist Factory in New York. Although women's contributions to the North's victory in the Civil War had won them praise, they were still paid far less than men for the same kinds of work.

dramatic and notorious of all was the March 25, 1911, Triangle Shirtwaist Company fire in New York City. The factory, which occupied a ten-story building, employed more than four hundred women. To this day no one knows what started the fire, which began on the eighth floor. Most of the women on the lower floors managed to escape, but those on the ninth story were trapped and could not escape. In desperation, some jumped out of windows and plummeted to their deaths on the sidewalk below. "The crowd yelled 'Don't jump!'" the *New York Times* reported, "but it was jump or be burned, the proof of which is found in the fact that fifty burned bodies were taken from the ninth floor alone."[28] In all, 146 people, mostly women, were killed.

> **"It was jump or be burned."[28]**
>
> —The *New York Times*, reporting on the Triangle factory fire

The catastrophe shocked and horrified people around the world, including large sectors of the American public. In New York City and across the nation, people demanded that both local

"A Mere Animal Existence"

Elizabeth Gurley Flynn was an activist who worked for the Industrial Workers of the World international labor union from 1907 to 1917. Shortly after the tragic Triangle factory fire in 1911, she published an article titled "Women in Industry Should Organize" in an industry trade journal. In this excerpt, she boldly makes the case that both traditional society and industry have come to brutalize many women, who often have to work outside the home just to survive.

> Women to the number of seven million have been driven forth from the home, by dire necessity, into the industrial arena, to be even more fiercely exploited than their brother workers. They are constantly seeking relief and release from the labor market on the marriage mart [market], which marks women the wage worker as a transitory [temporary] being; and the social or cooperative spirit engendered in the factory is usually neutralized by the struggle [to find] husbands [living] outside. Multitudes of wives and mothers are virtually sex slaves through their direct and debasing dependence upon individual men for their existence, and motherhood is all too often unwelcome and enforced, while the struggle for existence even in the homes where love [exists] is usually so fierce that life degenerates to a mere animal existence, a struggle for creature comforts. . . . How can one have depth or mental scope when one's life is spent exclusively within the four walls of one's individual composite home and workshop, performing personal service continually?

Elizabeth Gurley Flynn, "Women in Industry Should Organize," in *Words on Fire: The Life and Writing of Elizabeth Gurley Flynn*, ed. Rosalyn Fraad Baxandall. New Brunswick, NJ: Rutgers University Press, 1987, p. 92.

and national officials implement new workplace reforms. During the years that followed, therefore, much stricter safety laws were enacted in factories and other workplaces throughout America. These had a dramatic, positive effect on the lives of numerous working women.

Groups Supporting and Opposing Women's Suffrage

In the period in which these reforms were being implemented, the women's rights movement's other principal goal—gaining the right to vote—received more press coverage than ever. Some state legislatures began to respond to mounting pressure by women's groups, and by 1911, the year of the Triangle factory fire, five states had granted women suffrage—Colorado, Wyoming, Utah, Idaho, and Washington. Despite the lack of a federal law giving women voting rights, in the years that followed, more states joined this trend. They included Oregon, Arizona, Kansas, California, and Nevada, among others.

One reason for this positive development was that women's rights activists had learned the lesson that dividing their resources and working at cross-purposes only weakened their cause. In 1890 the two women's groups founded back in 1869 merged, forming the National American Woman Suffrage Association (NAWSA). The new organization significantly increased pressure on legislators to give women the vote. Trying to counter this effort were groups opposed to women's suffrage, whose members considered it a social threat. They believed that it would "destroy the family," one modern scholar explains, "and increase the number of socialist-leaning voters." In addition, many business leaders feared that "women would vote in favor of social and political reform,"[29] which might cost companies too much to institute.

However, these antisuffrage groups turned out to have little discernible effect on the women's suffrage movement, which continued to gain exposure. In March 1913, for instance, newspapers across the country covered a public demonstration by more than five thousand women, accompanied by nine marching bands, in Washington, DC. The organizer, attorney and social activist Inez Milholland, rode a horse in the parade's forefront. The suffrage movement also gained attention and credibility thanks to female contributions to US involvement in World War I (1914–1918). Hundreds of thousands of women did volunteer work, including some twenty thousand who served as nurses on the battlefields in France.

A Long Struggle Ends

At the war's height, meanwhile, a gallant female activist named Alice Paul established a radical new women's suffrage group—the

National Woman's Party (NWP). Members daringly picketed President Wilson's residence—the White House—in Washington, DC. At the time, such a move was widely seen as audacious, even disrespectful. In interviews, Paul compared the president to a homeowner dealing with creditors surrounding his house. "The man must either remove the creditors or pay the bill,"[30] she stated.

At first, local authorities took Paul at her word. They removed her and many of her colleagues and threw them in jail, where several female inmates suffered various illegal and cruel abuses. Even while this was happening, however, NAWSA increased pressure on President Wilson.

These efforts were ultimately successful, as Wilson came around and began securing political support for the women's

House Speaker Frederick Gillett signs the Nineteenth Amendment. Women's long struggle to gain the right to vote successfully concluded when the amendment went into effect on August 26, 1920.

vote in Congress and elsewhere behind the scenes. On January 10, 1918, the US House of Representatives passed a constitutional amendment allowing women's suffrage. The Senate voted against it at first. But on June 4, 1919, the senators voted again, this time passing the bill. The states then ratified what came to be known officially as the Nineteenth Amendment, which went into effect on August 26, 1920.

The vast majority of American women were overjoyed. Delighted suffragist Carrie Catt remarked about the long struggle, "How much of time and patience, how much work, energy, and aspiration, how much faith, how much hope, how much despair went into it."[31] One of her colleagues, Inez Irwin, described how the final generation of suffragists had been enlivened with "the spirit of youth." Bravely they had attacked the gates of politics and "forced them open," she said. Then, proudly, "they entered. And leaving behind all sinister remembrances of the battle, they turned their faces towards the morning."[32]

CHAPTER THREE

Battles for Recognition and Jobs

After American women finally acquired the right to vote in 1920, their position in society began to undergo several significant changes. First, a number of them ran for public office, some on the local level, others in state or even national elections. A fair number of female candidates lost those races. Yet a few succeeded in what had before been a strictly male domain. In 1921, for instance, Edna Beard became Vermont's first female legislator, serving first in the state's House of Representatives. In 1932 Hattie Caraway of Arkansas became the first woman elected to the US Senate, and in 1948 Maine's Margaret Chase Smith achieved the distinction of being the first woman elected to both the US Senate and House of Representatives (in separate years).

Besides these and other electoral firsts for American women, some others were appointed to high offices by sitting presidents. The most famous early example was Frances Perkins. In 1933 President Franklin D. Roosevelt chose her to be the US secretary of labor, making her the first woman to serve in a US presidential cabinet. The politically progressive Roosevelt also made Ruth Bryan Owen the first female ambassador to a foreign country (Denmark).

The Emergence of a New Public Woman

Despite these early achievements, most American politicians were still males. Yet for women, the political ice had finally been broken. Moreover, between 1920 and the early 1960s, American women made considerable strides in the social arena. Many historians have described the emergence of a so-called new public woman in the country, one who was far more likely than her mother had been to engage in a wide range of activities. These included wearing makeup regularly, dancing in public, drinking alcohol, and using swear words, to name only a few.

According to Emily Spivack of the Smithsonian Institution, the new American woman was shaped by a number of factors. These included "freedoms experienced from working outside the home, a push for equal rights, greater mobility, technological innovation and disposable income, [all of which] exposed [women] to new places, ideas and ways of living. Particularly for women, personal fulfillment and independence became priorities—a more modern, carefree spirit where anything seemed possible."[33]

Many people felt that the new, freer female image was reflected in the so-called flapper—a usually young, fun-loving woman

A group of young women show off beachwear that was in style in the early decades of the twentieth century. Many young women during the 1920s—often referred to as flappers—made a point of trying new things and testing traditional boundaries.

who was open to trying all sorts of new things. In 1922 popular flapper Zelda Fitzgerald explained how a typical flapper

> bobbed her hair, put on her choicest pair of earrings and a great deal of audacity and rouge and went into the battle. She flirted because it was fun to flirt and wore a one-piece bathing suit because she had a good figure, she covered her face with powder and paint [and] refused to be bored chiefly because she wasn't boring. [In addition] mothers disapproved of their sons taking the flapper to dances, to teas, to swim, and most of all to heart.[34]

The carefree flapper image seemed to echo the upbeat, optimistic outlook of the 1920s in America. There was a general rise in economic prosperity, particularly for the middle and upper classes. The era earned nicknames such as the Jazz Age—a term coined by writer F. Scott Fitzgerald, Zelda's husband—and the Roaring Twenties, in part because cities were rapidly expanding and featured a raft of public entertainments, among them jazz concerts, nightclubs, and dance marathons. Many women wanted to take part in these activities alongside men.

> "[The flapper] flirted because it was fun to flirt and wore a one-piece bathing suit because she had a good figure."[34]
>
> —Flapper Zelda Fitzgerald

Not all women of that period, however, were flappers. Indeed, flappers were only the proverbial cutting edge of female society. Most women remained struggling members of the middle and lower classes. Quite a few endured hardships, including having trouble making ends meet, a scarcity of good-paying jobs, and stress. Female retail clerks, historian Sara M. Evans points out, had a hard time smiling at the rich women who bought expensive goods from them, items that the salesgirls themselves could not afford to purchase. Also, she says, "racist hiring policies prevented many black women [from] experiencing the economic fruits of an expanding service sector. [They] found themselves forced into a very narrow range of job opportunities,"[35] such as maids and cooks.

Were Working Women a Menace to Society?

Whether a woman was well-off or poor and struggling during the Jazz Age, she could at least fall back on the knowledge that, unlike her mother, she could vote. Many of the women who had fought so hard to gain that right now felt content about their status and assumed that the struggle for women's rights was basically

"The Badge of Flapperhood"

In this excerpt from "A Flapper's Appeal to Parents," published in the December 1922 issue of *Outlook* magazine, a young flapper named Ellen Welles Page explained some of what being a flapper was about.

If one judges by appearances, I suppose I am a flapper. I am within the age limit. I wear bobbed hair, the badge of flapperhood. (And, oh, what a comfort it is!) I powder my nose. I wear fringed skirts and bright-colored sweaters, and scarves, and waists [shirts] with Peter Pan collars, and low-heeled "finale hopper" shoes. I adore to dance. I spend a large amount of time in automobiles. I attend hops [dances], and proms, and ball-games, and crew races, and other affairs at men's colleges. . . . There are many degrees of flapper. There is the semi-flapper; the flapper; the super-flapper. Each of these three main general divisions has its degrees of variation. I might possibly be placed somewhere in the middle of the first class. I want to beg all you parents, and grandparents, and friends, and teachers, and preachers— you who constitute the "older generation"—to overlook our shortcomings, at least for the present, and to appreciate our virtues. I wonder if it ever occurred to any of you that it required brains to become and remain a successful flapper? Indeed it does! It requires an enormous amount of cleverness and energy to keep going at the proper pace. It requires self-knowledge and self-analysis. We must know our capabilities and limitations.

Quoted in Emily Spivack, "The History of the Flapper, Part 1: A Call to Freedom," *Smithsonian*, February 5, 2013. www.smithsonianmag.com.

over. Illustrating that new complacency was the NAWSA, which in 1920 changed its name to the League of Women Voters. Its primary goal now was to train young women to be good citizens and vote whenever possible.

A smaller number of women, however, were not nearly so content with the new female lot in life. Alice Paul and other members of the National Woman's Party, for example, felt that the fight for women's rights was in many ways just beginning. Women were still second-class citizens in numerous ways, they said, and they must fight to change that.

At first, an important way to bring about such social change seemed to be by another constitutional amendment, one that directly addressed the issue of female equality. Molded and pushed by various women's rights activists, it became known as the Equal Rights Amendment (ERA). The original version, penned by Paul herself, stated that women should enjoy equal rights with men. There was initially a good deal of opposition to it from male politicians. In part, this was because male business owners worried that if it passed, they would have to raise women's salaries to match those of their male employees. For this and other reasons, when Congress first examined the ERA in 1923, its mostly male members refused to even vote on it.

In any case, such protective legislation for women soon became a moot point. In 1929 a dramatic change in the country's economy suddenly dealt the women's rights movement a staggering blow that nearly halted its forward momentum. That year the national stock market crashed and sent the country, along with most of the rest of the world, into a downward financial spiral. The so-called Great Depression that followed held society in its crippling grip throughout the 1930s. The US unemployment rate had stood at a mere 3 percent just before the crash. By 1933 it was a shocking 25 percent overall, and for African Americans it was as high as 50 percent.

At the time at least 99 percent of American women were either middle class or poor. Many, along with their children, soon became homeless, and even those who managed to stay in their houses did not regularly have enough to eat. It became common to see women selling apples on street corners. Others stood in long lines each day to receive a loaf of bread supplied by a local charity. One charity worker later recalled seeing a distressed woman who cruised the local docks "and picked up vegetables that fell from the wagons. Sometimes the fish vendors gave her fish at the end of the day. On two different occasions, her family was without food for a day and a half. [Another] family did not have food for two days. Then the husband went out and gathered dandelions and the family lived on them."[36]

> "The husband went out and gathered dandelions and the family lived on them."[36]
>
> —A 1930s charity worker's description of a poor family

Making the plight of American women even worse during the Depression era was a widespread attitude that women who managed to find work were a menace to society because they were taking jobs away from men. This attitude led to a great deal of discrimination against women. During the middle to late 1930s, two-thirds of US banks and utility companies and three-quarters of insurance companies refused to hire women for any position. Under these dire conditions, most American women could do little but simply try to survive; they could not seriously consider spending many hours per week fighting for social equality.

Female Role Models in Government and the Military

Incredibly, however, during the Depression era a small group of dedicated, hardworking women did break some new ground for their gender. Most had been suffragists and therefore knew how to organize to achieve political goals. One of these women was Frances Perkins, whom President Roosevelt had chosen to tackle various social problems. Perkins became one of the guiding forces in the creation of the Social Security system, which delivered badly needed financial aid to families beginning in 1935. Another key Roosevelt appointee, Mary McLeod Bethune, was the first African American woman to head a US agency. In directing the Office of Minority Affairs, she used intelligence and hard work to overcome entrenched social biases and discrimination, becoming a role model for other women.

An even more prominent role model for female social advancement was Roosevelt's wife, Eleanor. In her unique position as the nation's First Lady, she urged her husband to hire as many women as possible. She also opened the White House to women with new ideas for making the government run more smoothly. In addition, to give women reporters more opportunities and public visibility, Eleanor limited press coverage of her own activities to female reporters. That inspired a new generation of young women to study journalism and become newspaper reporters and editors.

The Roosevelts were still very much at the forefront of American government and life when the United States entered World War II in 1941. American women once more found themselves challenged by a wartime society and economy. As they had during World War I, in the new conflict they took many of the factory and business jobs left vacant by men who went off to fight. In all, more than 18 million American women worked outside the home during World War II, some 3 million of them in industries that made weapons and other war-related products.

To attract as many women as possible to such jobs, the government sponsored ad campaigns. The most famous example featured the tough, resourceful fictional character Rosie the Riveter, created by artist J. Howard Miller. In most of the ads, Rosie held up her right arm and flexed her bicep—a typically male gesture that symbolized getting down to work.

In addition to the women who took on men's jobs during the war, some 350,000 women actually served in the military. These

This poster, created by J. Howard Miller, was designed to boost the morale of American women who worked in factories that manufactured munitions during World War II.

women performed the important work of electricians, mechanics, radio operators, weather forecasters, cryptologists (code breakers), parachute riggers, aerial photography analysts, and nurses. In virtually every instance, the women who served in the military performed in an exemplary manner. This went far in changing male attitudes about supposedly weak and unskilled women.

The Ideal Woman of the 1950s

In fact, the image of energetic, highly effective working women during the war, both inside and outside the military, turned out to be a lasting one. It became a major factor in the revival of the women's rights movement just after midcentury. That revival did not happen immediately following the war's conclusion, however. Instead, it was delayed by a new, far-reaching social trend—the baby boom. At war's end, historian Elaine T. May writes, large numbers of working women "lost their wartime positions to the returning [male]

A Conspiracy to Keep Women in the Home

Betty Friedan's book *The Feminine Mystique* was published in 1963 and quickly became a best seller, with more than a million copies sold in the first year alone. In the book Friedan challenged the existing system in which the highest aspiration of women was said, mostly by men, to be a mother and housewife. She concluded that this was an artificial construct imposed on women by what she called the "manipulators." These were a collection of sources—including women's magazines, a slanted women's educational system, and media advertisers—that together conspired to pigeonhole women in the role of housewife and to make them lose their own identities in the process. The owners of large-scale businesses, she said, are the most powerful of the perpetrators because

> it is their millions which blanket the land with persuasive images, flattering the American housewife, diverting her guilt and disguising her growing sense of emptiness. They have done this so successfully, employing the techniques and concepts of modern social science, and transposing them into those deceptively simple, clever, outrageous ads and commercials, that an observer of the American scene today accepts as fact that the great majority of American women have no ambition other than to be housewives. If they are not solely responsible for sending women home, they are surely responsible for keeping them there. [They] have seared the feminine mystique deep into every woman's mind and into the minds of her husband, her children, her neighbors.

Betty Friedan, *The Feminine Mystique*. New York: Norton, 1963, pp. 31–32.

veterans. Men and women alike were expected to [give up] their emergency roles and settle into domestic life." In that new societal dynamic, men were viewed as the breadwinners and women as the homemakers. So, May continues, "there was no room for the independent single woman, nor the career married woman."[37]

In the postwar America of the late 1940s and on into the 1950s, the economy was strong, and most men had jobs. Therefore, society no longer saw a pressing need for large numbers of women to go to work. As a result, a lot of women stayed home and concentrated on building families, and that created the baby boom.

During this period, lasting roughly from 1945 to 1960, large numbers of Americans imagined themselves to be part of a broad social ideal. They consistently saw it play out in the programs produced for the new electronic medium of television. That ideal was one of a comfortable middle-class, usually all-white family that was happy and free from major strife. *Father Knows Best* and *Leave It to Beaver* typified the new model of American life. It featured the ideal woman as a low-key, friendly mother who primarily cooked and cleaned, almost always decked out with a formal dress, perfectly coiffed hair, and a set of pearls.

> **"There was no room for the independent single woman, nor the career married woman."[37]**
>
> —Historian Elaine T. May on the postwar American family

A Major Upsurge in Female Activism

These bland, mildly entertaining television shows conveniently ignored the more troubling realities of American life. These included poverty, extreme racism against African Americans, and sexism that continued to cast most women in social roles considered inferior to those of men. As time went on, at least some women saw the homemaker image popularized on television as outdated, not to mention inaccurate.

In fact, all through the 1950s increasing numbers of women obtained jobs. Either their families needed them to earn extra income or the women felt that working outside the home made them feel more fulfilled. In 1950 about 25 percent of American women held outside jobs; by 1960 that figure had risen to 39 percent. Moreover, despite the baby boom, women in the 1950s had fewer children than their mothers had. By 1960 women "also married younger," Evans points out, "and concentrated their childbearing in the early years of marriage."[38] Thus, by the early 1960s it was becoming more and more the norm for women to work outside the home.

With these facts in mind, when the young, progressive politician John F. Kennedy was elected US president in 1960, some influential women saw his ascendancy as an opportunity for women to continue their fight for equal rights. At their urging, he established a study group—the Presidential Commission on the Status of Women. The commission issued its findings in 1963. Women faced discrimination in employment, it said, as well as unequal pay and a severe lack of child care services.

In response, Kennedy pushed a bill called the Equal Pay Act (EPA) through Congress. It forbade employers to pay women less than men for the same job. At that moment in time, American women earned about fifty-nine cents for each dollar a man earned; thanks in part to the EPA, by 1970 that ratio had risen to sixty-two cents per dollar. The smallness of the increase was attributed to a general lack of enforcement of the law. Upset over that, female activists saw clearly that there was still a long way to go before women achieved real equality.

> "To bring women into full participation in the mainstream of American society."[39]
>
> —A stated goal of the National Organization for Women

The result was a new upsurge in women fighting for their rights. It was to some degree spearheaded by the formation of the National Organization for Women (NOW) in 1966 by best-selling author Betty Friedan. NOW's initial statement of intent declared that its purpose was "to bring women into full participation in the mainstream of American society" and to achieve "truly equal partnership with men."[39]

On June 10, 1963 President John F. Kennedy signed the Equal Pay Act, which prohibited employers from paying women less than men for the same work.

This resurgence of feminism during the 1960s, Stanford University scholar Estelle B. Freedman says, "revived questions about protective legislation." Feminists across the country now increasingly pushed for new laws "prohibiting discrimination in hiring, pay, and training."[40] The best legislation to accomplish that goal, the activists said, was the ERA crafted back in the 1920s. Congress had looked at it several times over the ensuing decades but had never passed it. The question was whether the men who still overwhelmingly controlled the US government would finally pass that controversial legislation. If they did, the lives of American women were sure to change forever.

CHAPTER FOUR

Striving for True Equality

Historians, female activists, and others who have closely followed the progress of the women's rights movement over time often speak of feminism's so-called second wave. The first wave, they agree, consisted of the many advancements of American women leading up to the achievement of female suffrage in 1920. The second wave is generally defined as beginning with the resurgence of the fight for women's rights during the 1960s and 1970s.

To the general public, however, those newer women's advancements were collectively better known as women's liberation, or women's lib for short. As had occurred during feminism's first wave, between the 1960s and the 1980s increasing numbers of women contributed some measure of time and/or energy to the cause. Some marched in the streets, picketed, or took part in sit-ins, in which they called attention to the cause by sitting down inside public buildings or private businesses and refusing to leave, forcing the police to remove them. Other women protested by writing to or phoning their representatives in Congress and demanding they support women's rights. Some wrote letters to their local newspapers. Still others more quietly, but no less importantly, made financial contributions to women's organizations like NOW.

Millions of American women were happy about the many strides the women's liberation movement made during these years. Yet not all women were pleased with their social and political progress. A minority of American women actually disapproved of feminism, the women's liberation movement, and most efforts to make women equal with men.

One of the leaders of this countermovement was conservative attorney and writer Phyllis Schlafly. She suggested that feminists were bitter, unhappy individuals with many personal problems who

Women march down New York City's Fifth Avenue in April 1970 as part of a nationwide demonstration for women's liberation.

protested and sought to change laws mainly to make themselves feel better. Those who fought for women's lib, Schlafly said, were sick people who saw their homes as jails and viewed wives and mothers, supposedly the bedrock of traditional society, as slaves. The women's liberation movement, she asserted, "is a total assault on the role of the American woman as wife and mother, and on the family as the basic unit of society." The female protesters "are promoting day care centers for babies instead of homes," she continued. "They are promoting abortions instead of families."[41]

> "[The women's liberation movement] is a total assault on the role of the American woman as wife and mother."[41]
>
> —Antifeminist activist Phyllis Schlafly

A Banner Year

One reason why Schlafly and those who agreed with her spoke out both loudly and repeatedly was because the women's liberation movement slowly but steadily achieved various successes during this pivotal period. "The upheavals of the second wave period left their mark," a spokesperson for the National Woman's Party points out. "Changes—legal, economic, political, and social—were real, and appeared to be unchallengeable."[42]

On the political front, for example, in 1971 best-selling author Betty Friedan, congresswomen Bella Abzug and Shirley Chisholm, noted journalist Gloria Steinem, and some other feminist colleagues founded the National Women's Political Caucus (NWPC). It was and remains a nonpartisan group—that is, it is open to members of all political parties. An important goal of the NWPC is to find, train, and support feminist-minded women who will run for public office. It is understood that once such a candidate is elected, she will fight for improved education for women as well as for new laws that will protect women from discrimination. Today the NWPC continues to promote these and other pro-woman policies.

Also, in 1972 the versatile Steinem helped women achieve a fuller, stronger voice on the social front by publishing the first national feminist magazine, *Ms.* (The term had only recently been coined by feminists to replace the titles *Mrs.* and *Miss*, which define marital status. These feminists felt that since men had a title that did not indicate marital status—*Mr.*—women should have one, too.) The new magazine proved to be a huge success. It often educated the public about important issues relating to the lives of women of all walks of life. According to one of Steinem's biographers, "Its initial publication of 300,000 copies sold out rapidly nationwide. The magazine became the landmark publication of the feminist movement. Unlike other women's magazines of the time, *Ms.* covered topics such as gender bias in language, sexual harassment, feminist protest of pornography, and political candidates' stances on women's issues."[43]

In addition, the early 1970s featured a number of female-related legal advances that permanently altered American women's lives. Continuing as a banner year for women, 1972 witnessed Congress's passage of the Equal Employment Opportunity Act. Among its multiple provisions was the establishment of the Equal Employment Opportunity Commission (EEOC), which investigates claims of discrimination in workplaces across the nation. If this agency finds that such a claim has merit, it can sue the employer in question in federal court. Thousands of women began to find legal redress from biases in hiring during the agency's first year alone.

Helping Women Obtain Credit

Congress passed many new laws pertaining to women and their issues during the pivotal decade of the 1970s, including the Equal Employment Opportunity Act and the 1973 Supreme Court ruling that legalized abortion. Another important new law affecting women from that period was the Equal Credit Opportunity Act (ECOA), described here by the Consumer Financial Protection Bureau.

> ECOA was passed at a time when discrimination against women applying for credit was common. For example, mortgage lenders often discounted a married woman's income, especially if she was of childbearing age. Things weren't much better for single women, either. Organizations that lobbied for the passage of ECOA also claimed that mortgage lenders were more likely to deny credit to single women relative to other applicants.
>
> Congress originally passed ECOA in October of 1974. When it was enacted, ECOA prohibited lending discrimination based on sex or marital status.
>
> Not long after the original law was passed, in March of 1976 Congress amended the law to further prohibit lending discrimination based on race, color, religion, national origin, age, the receipt of public assistance income, or exercising one's rights under certain consumer protection laws.

Brian Kreiswirth and Anna Marie Tabor, "What You Need to Know About the Equal Credit Opportunity Act and How It Can Help You: Why It Was Passed and What It Is," Consumer Financial Protection Bureau, October 31, 2016. www.consumerfinance.gov.

Still another legal advance of 1972 was Title IX, a piece of legislation that prohibited discrimination in all educational institutions that receive federal money. This meant that most schools could no longer place limits on the number of women accepted for certain programs, such as the study of medicine or law. Title IX also required schools to offer young women equal chances with young men to play various sports. The long-range effects of Title IX were "simply phenomenal," historians Bonnie Eisenberg and Mary Ruthsdotter explain:

> "The whole world saw how much American women athletes could achieve."[44]
>
> —Historians Bonnie Eisenberg and Mary Ruthsdotter

The number of women doctors, lawyers, engineers, architects and other professionals doubled and doubled again as quotas actually limiting women's enrollment in graduate schools were outlawed. Athletics [was] probably the most hotly contested area of Title IX, and it [was] one of the hottest areas of improvement, too. The rise in girls' and women's participation in athletics tells the story: One in twenty-seven high school girls played sports [in 1973]; [more than] one in three do today. The whole world saw how much American women athletes could achieve during the last few Olympic Games, measured in their astonishing numbers of gold, silver, and bronze medals. This was another very visible result of Title IX.[44]

Defeat Offset by Victory

The early 1970s also finally saw some movement on a piece of legislation that members of the women's rights movement had been pushing for decades. Strongly pressured by NOW and other women's organizations, the US Congress passed the Equal Rights Amendment. This win for feminists was doubly impressive because the antifeminists had lobbied hard to stop its passage.

Schlafly, for instance, had warned that making the ERA law would deprive women of alimony and child support in divorce cases. She also claimed that women would immediately be drafted into the military and be forced into combat positions. In addition, Schlafly said, the ERA was an affront to God, who had created women specifically to have babies and take care of the family home. "It's simply the way God made us,"[45] she stated. Since no evidence existed to support any of these claims, Congress ignored Schlafly and her followers and passed the amendment.

In the end, however, Schlafly and her supporters were able to block the ratification of the ERA. As happens with every constitutional amendment that passes Congress, the proposed new law had to be ratified by a minimum of thirty-eight of the fifty states.

A minority of American women opposed women's liberation. Phyllis Schafly (center) opposed the movement that she considered to be "an assault on the role of the American woman as wife and mother and on the family as the basic unit of society."

In 1982, having taken ten years to make the rounds of the state legislatures, the amendment fell short by three states and failed to go into effect. Continued scare tactics and false claims by Schlafly and her ilk were widely credited with damaging the ratification process. Also, only 46 percent of male state legislators voted for passage, and they largely controlled the states' lawmaking apparatus.

In the wake of the ERA's failure to become the law, American feminists were extremely disappointed. However, most of them considered that this defeat had been partially offset by an enor-

The Family and Medical Leave Act

Thanks to the growing number of women who entered Congress during the 1990s, legislation that particularly benefited women began passing more frequently than in the past. The historian of the House of Representatives, Matthew Wasniewski, describes one of the more important of these new laws and includes an anecdote revealing how male legislators tried to take credit for the efforts of their female colleagues.

One of the most heralded pieces of legislation initiated by women in Congress—notably, Patricia Schroeder and Marge Roukema—was the Family and Medical Leave Act. Passed by Congress in February 1993, this measure required employers to grant employees up to 12 weeks of unpaid leave each year for a chronic health problem, for the birth or adoption of a child, or for the care of a family member with a serious illness. Some Congresswomen observed afterward that men were quick to take credit for an issue that women had pushed initially and consistently. At the presidential bill-signing ceremony, only male Senators and Representatives shared the stage with President Clinton.

Schroeder, who was seated in the audience, later commented on the absence of recognition for the work of women legislators. She observed, "Often you see women start the issue, educate on the issue, fight for the issue, and then when it becomes fashionable, men push us aside," Schroeder observed, "and they get away with it."

Matthew Wasniewski, "Forging Lasting Institutional Change," History, Art & Archives, US House of Representatives, Office of the Historian. http://history.house.gov.

mous victory for women that had occurred shortly after Congress had passed the ERA. In 1973, in a case titled *Roe v. Wade*, the US Supreme Court made a landmark ruling on abortion. Before that time all forms of abortion had been against federal law, although a few states had shortly before begun to grant limited abortion rights. In a seven-to-two vote, the high court determined that women should not be denied the right to make this very personal decision involving both their privacy and their own bodies. According to USHistory.org,

> The majority of the justices maintained that a right to privacy was implied by the Ninth and Fourteenth Amendments. No state could restrict abortions during the first three months, or trimester, of a pregnancy. States were permitted to adopt restrictive laws in accordance with respecting the mother's health during the second trimester. The practice could be banned outright during the third trimester. Any state law that conflicted with this ruling was automatically overturned.[46]

New Challenges and the Year of the Woman

The Supreme Court decision in *Roe v. Wade* was controversial at the time, and it remains so today. Yet throughout the intervening years it has also been deemed appropriate by a majority of American women and men: a 2016 Pew Research Center poll found that 69 percent of Americans want to see *Roe v. Wade* maintained. Along with the NWPC, the EEOC, Title IX, and other advances made on behalf of women during the 1970s, the 1973 abortion ruling became a permanent part of America's social landscape. Thanks to the efforts of untold numbers of dedicated activists in feminism's second wave, women had fought for what they saw as their rights and had created real change.

Those accomplishments reflected "the increasing power women [had] amassed,"[47] says scholar Ellen Fitzpatrick. The burning question was whether the women's rights movement would continue to maintain and even increase that newfound power. There was widespread worry among feminists that their forward momentum could not be maintained unless more women got involved in politics on both the local and national levels. As a result of this realization of what needed to be done, thousands of "younger women set out to update feminism to meet" new challenges, Duke University scholar Nancy MacLean writes. "The first generation born in the wake of the women's movement's greatest victories came in the 1990s" and included increased "voter registration campaigns to draw young women into politics."[48]

The first important step in this attempt to widen women's role in America's political processes took place in 1984. At the national convention held by the Democratic Party for that year's upcoming presidential election, New York lawyer Geraldine Ferraro was nominated as Walter Mondale's running mate. Although Mondale lost to Ronald Reagan in the ensuing election, the fact that a woman had appeared on the national ballot as a vice presidential candidate was significant. It symbolized the steadily changing political atmosphere for American women.

Indeed, increasing numbers of women who had never before run for public office now began to do so. Some of them lost their races, but others won. This trend reached its first climax in 1992, which thereafter became known as the Year of the Woman. The historian of the US House of Representatives, Matthew Wasniewski, recalls,

> In 1992 women went to the polls energized by a record-breaking number of women on the federal ticket. Nationally, 11 women won major party nominations for Senate races while 106 women contended for House seats in the general election. The results were unprecedented. The 24 women who won election to the U.S. House of Repre-

sentatives for the first time that November comprised the largest number elected to the House in any single election, and the three women elected to the Senate tripled the number of women in that chamber.[49]

The Year of the Woman, Wasniewski notes, also marked the start of more than twenty years of noteworthy accomplishments for minority women. In fact, forty-seven of the fifty-eight Hispanic American, African American, and Asian Pacific American women who have been members of Congress were elected between 1992 and 2016. One of these minority women—Carol Mosley Braun—was the first African American woman to serve in the US Senate.

Some of the other women elected in 1992, including a few of the minority members, had political experience, as they had served in city or state government before running for national office. For example, Wasniewski explains,

> "In 1992 women went to the polls energized by a record-breaking number of women on the federal ticket."[49]
>
> —House of Representatives historian Matthew Wasniewski

long before her election to the U.S. House, Eva Clayton was active in the civil rights movement and served as the assistant secretary of the North Carolina department of natural resources and community development. When she arrived in Congress, Clayton became the state's first African-American Representative since 1901. [She] saw her time in state government as an important stepping stone toward a seat in Congress, giving her "a feel for the interrelationship between state and federal government."[50]

Female Roles in Government Expand

These political gains for women in Congress were part of a larger, ongoing expansion of female roles in the US government. It had

In 2016 Hillary Rodham Clinton became the first woman presidential nominee of either of America's major political parties.

begun before the Year of the Woman—when, in 1981, President Reagan had nominated the first female Supreme Court justice. Distinguished Stanford Law School graduate and Arizona judge Sandra Day O'Connor was confirmed for the position unanimously by the members of the Senate. More nominations of women to the high court followed. In 1993 President Bill Clinton named District of Columbia Court of Appeals judge Ruth Bader Ginsburg. In 2009, President Barack Obama nominated Second Circuit Court of Appeals judge Sonia Sotomayor; the following year, Obama nominated Harvard Law School dean and US solicitor general Elena Kagan. When Kagan joined the high court, for the first time ever one-third of its justices were women.

Meanwhile, in 2007, two years before Sotomayor's nomination, a woman became part of the immediate line of succession to the US presidency. That year California congresswoman Nancy Pelosi became the sixtieth—and first female—Speaker of the House of Representatives. This elevation put her second in line, after the vice president, to become president if both the president and vice president were somehow unable to serve.

In 2008 former First Lady and US senator Hillary Rodham Clinton made history as well. In a bid for the presidency, she won the New Hampshire primary, becoming the first woman to win a presidential primary. Later that year, fellow Democrat Barack Obama narrowly defeated her for the party's nomination and went on to become the first African American to win the presidency. Almost immediately after his victory, Obama announced that Clinton would serve as his secretary of state, the most prestigious US cabinet post. She served in that office for the next four years.

In 2016 Clinton became the first woman ever to win a major party nomination for the presidency. In the election in early November, she won the popular vote by a commanding margin—65.8 million (48 percent) to 62.9 million (46 percent). However, because her opponent Donald Trump received roughly seventy thousand more votes than she did in three key states, he won the Electoral College vote and, with it, the presidency. Clinton's defeat saddened her many female supporters. Yet some of them managed to take heart, seeing her nearly successful campaign alone as a positive sign for the future of American women. "Maybe this election was the beginning of something new," suggested Lindy West, a columnist for the popular online newspaper the *Guardian*. Perhaps, she added, it was "not the death of sexism, but the birth of a world in which women's inferiority isn't a given."[51]

> "Maybe this election was the beginning of something new."[51]
>
> —*Guardian* columnist Lindy West on the 2016 presidential race

CHAPTER FIVE

The Struggle for Equality Goes On

Over the course of more than a century and a half, the American women's rights movement has had a profound impact not only on women's lives and rights but also on society as a whole. What is sometimes called the feminist revolution has employed a wide range of tactics to effect this change. As scholar Estelle B. Freedman says, these have included grassroots protests, the flourishing of women's literature and art, female participation in athletics, and the election of women to public office both locally and nationally. Through these and other means, she remarks, "the past generation has expanded the reach of feminism enormously."[52]

Yet no feminist, historian, or other close observer of these trends has any illusion that women have managed to attain true equality with men. Indeed, women continue to struggle for equality in many social areas. Among the more publicized recent examples have been obstacles to female service in the American military, continued efforts by women to receive the same pay as men for the same work, and the upsurge of women of all social levels courageously going public with their harrowing experiences of sexual harassment.

On the surface, these and similar areas of contention between women and a still partly sexist society may appear daunting and disheartening. Yet as Freedman and some other feminists point out, they have a positive side as well. Namely, they show that large numbers of women refuse to give up their battle for equality. In the future, she predicts, the women's rights movement "will continue to redefine its politics and broaden its reach." This fight "to recognize all women as fully human and fully citizens, to value women's labors as much as men's, [continues] to expand."[53]

Changing the Military Forever

The courage displayed by women who refused to knuckle under to long-entrenched male social dominance is nowhere more impressive than in the experiences of young women trying to enter the military. Scholar Nancy MacLean calls it "the most avidly masculine institution in American life." During the 1990s and the decade that followed, the various branches of the US military were flooded with thousands of female applicants. Joining up during this period was "especially important to African American women and Latinas," MacLean points out. They enlisted "in the military in large numbers in hopes of education funding and social mobility."[54]

This influx of young women joining the military changed that institution forever. The effects of the change became evident almost

The first two decades of the twenty-first century have seen increasing numbers of American women joining the military. Starting in 2015, the US military allowed women to serve in most combat roles.

right away. In 1970 only around 2 percent of US military personnel were female. By the advent of the Persian Gulf War of the early 1990s, however, that percentage had more than tripled to 7 percent. More than forty thousand women served in combat support in that conflict, and sixteen of them were killed in the line of duty. Moreover, the number of women serving their country continued to grow.

Between 2001 and 2010, more than 235,000 women served in US operations in Iraq and Afghanistan, some of them in combat roles. The latter cases were unofficial because women were still legally prohibited from fighting on the front lines at the time. That barrier also fell, however, when, in 2015, the US military officially began allowing women to take part in most combat roles.

Women at the Military Academies

All of those women who eagerly served—whether in combat or noncombat jobs—had to be trained, of course. Some simply enlisted and received regular training in one military branch or another. However, increasing numbers of women opted to attend one of the several esteemed military academies that produce young officers—for instance, the army's US Military Academy in West Point, New York, and the US Naval Academy in Annapolis, Maryland.

South Carolina's Citadel—one of the six leading military academies in the country—became the focus of much attention in 1995. That year a young woman named Shannon Faulkner became the first female to attend the school. She had been turned down when she first applied, specifically because of her gender, and had resorted to going to court to gain admission. In part because of severe harassment by male cadets, Faulkner left the Citadel after only a week. But she had in a real sense opened the door there to other women. In 1996 the school regularly started admitting women. The first of them to graduate, in 1999, was Nancy Mace. When asked how she and other female cadets had changed the Citadel, she proudly replied, "for the better."[55]

A Black Woman's Success at West Point

Founded in 1802, the US Military Academy at West Point is America's oldest service academy. White women began to be accepted there in small numbers during the 1970s. Later in that decade African American women started to gain admission there as well. In 1980 Pat Locke was one of the first two African American women to graduate from the academy. Both white and minority women applied to West Point in even larger numbers during the 1980s, 1990s, and the decades that followed. At first, most male cadets assumed that only men would be able to rise to the prestigious position of first captain of the entire corps of cadets—a person commanding all forty-four hundred of them. But those who made this assumption were proved wrong. In 1989 Kristin Baker became the first woman to attain that coveted rank. Later, in 2017, twenty-one-year-old Simone Askew was the first African American woman to become West Point's first captain. In an interview for CBS News, Askew said, "My focus now is really to be the best first captain I can be regardless of gender or race, and [that] I'm remembered as a good leader and not necessarily as a good African-American female leader." In a 2017 interview, Locke remarked about Askew, "You see so much of our nation in her. The way that she thinks, the way that she carries herself. She knows she wants to be a leader because she wants to make a difference."

Quoted in CBS News, "Profiles in Service: West Point Cadet Simone Askew on Making History and Leadership," December 25, 2017. www.cbsnews.com.

A few other military academies, including the US Air Force Academy in Colorado, which first admitted female cadets in 1976, experienced a similar sequence of events. At first there was some harassment of the female cadets, but it was soon followed by their general acceptance. To the dismay of many Americans, however, resentment against women entering a traditionally male domain did not disappear completely. Between 2015 and 2017 harassment of female cadets resurfaced at the US Air Force Academy. In late 2017 CBS and other news outlets broke the story of sexual assaults against some of the academy's female cadets, including Emily Hazen and Melissa Hildremyr. The two said that they reported their sexual assaults to academy officials, but those leaders blamed the victims and did nothing to stop the abuse. Hildremyr told the media how those who ran the school took the side of the male cadets who had assaulted her. The officials, she said, "would say things like, 'These guys have every reason to tell the truth and you have every reason to lie.' And they [made] me feel like it was my fault this had happened to me."[56]

Seeking Equal Wages

In late 2017 and early 2018, officers higher in the air force ranks announced they were in the midst of a thorough investigation of the harassment complaints the young women had filed. In the

meantime, several newspaper and television editors commented that they were not surprised by the allegations. True, they pointed out, women had made enormous social and political strides in recent decades. But their long struggle for equality goes on because they are not yet on a completely even playing field with men in many areas.

Another of those areas, the commentators said, is the workplace, especially regarding the issue of how women are paid for their work. In 2010 national surveys found that, on average, women earned just over seventy cents for every dollar made by a man for the same work. The proportion was even lower for minority women. At the time, black women were making sixty-four cents and Hispanic women fifty-two cents for each male dollar. Various studies showed that the Equal Pay Act and other similar laws designed to close the earning gap between the genders had definitely helped over time. Yet though smaller, that gap still existed, most likely because those laws were often not evenly or strictly enforced.

Typical of this continuing wage discrimination were the experiences of Lilly Ledbetter, who worked for many years at a tire factory in Alabama. In 1999 she compared her paycheck to that of a male coworker and saw that he made 15 percent more than she did for performing the same work. After thinking about it for

In January 2009 President Barack Obama signed the Lilly Ledbetter Act, which eliminates the time limitation for women to file complaints about wage discrimination.

a while, she complained to her boss and asked for a raise; when he refused, she sued the company. The jury found in her favor and told the company to pay her $224,000 in lost wages. But the company appealed the decision, and the case eventually went to the Supreme Court. The justices ruled against Ledbetter because, they said, she had complained to her boss too late. By law, she should have done so within the first 180 days after receiving her inequitable paycheck.

Ledbetter was to some degree vindicated, however. A few years later, in 2009, President Obama signed into law the Lilly Ledbetter Fair Pay Act, named for her. It eliminated the 180-day clause in the existing laws. Five years later, in 2014, the National Women's Law Center in Washington, DC, evaluated the

Anita Hill's Gripping Testimony

A few years before the 1991 Senate Judiciary Committee hearings on Clarence Thomas's nomination to the US Supreme Court, Thomas was Anita Hill's supervisor at the Equal Employment Opportunity Commission. In her testimony to the senators regarding Thomas, Hill said, "After approximately three months of working there, he asked me to go out socially with him." This, Hill claimed, was the start of a long series of incidents of sexual harassment. She went on, saying in part,

> I declined the invitation to go out socially with him, and explained to him that I thought it would jeopardize what at the time I considered to be a very good working relationship. I had a normal social life with other men outside the office. I believed then, as now, that having a social relationship with a person who is supervising my work would be ill advised. I was very uncomfortable with the idea and told him so. I thought that by saying no and explaining my reasons, my employer would abandon his social suggestions. However, to my regret, in the following few weeks, he continued to ask me out on several occasions. He pressed me to justify my reasons for saying no to him. These incidents took place in his office, or mine. They were in the form of private conversations, which would not have been overheard by anyone else. My working relationship became even more strained when Judge Thomas began to use work situations to discuss sex.

Quoted in Miriam Schneir, ed., *Feminism in Our Time: The Essential Writings, World War II to the Present.* New York: Random House, 1994, pp. 73–74.

new law's impact. Regarding a person's right to complain to or sue an employer without time limitations, the organization says, "The Ledbetter Act has already made a critical difference for the workers whose rights were [gutted] by the Ledbetter decision. It restored the ability of workers in all occupations and parts of the country to seek to vindicate their rights against pay discrimination."[57]

The law's actual effect on women's wages has been minimal, however. This can be seen in the data on wages the government keeps track of each year. By 2017 American women made an average of seventy-seven cents for every dollar a man earned, about five or six cents more than in 2010. The reality, legal and financial experts say, is that full wage-earning parity between men and women will likely take several more years to achieve. The National Women's Law Center explains why advances in this area continue to occur slowly:

> Our existing equal pay laws remain weakened by a series of other court decisions that have opened loopholes in the law and by insufficient federal tools to detect and combat pay discrimination. In addition, too often wage disparities go undetected because employers maintain policies that punish employees who voluntarily share salary information with their coworkers.[58]

Various Workplace Biases

Unequal pay among female and male workers is not the only workplace problem that women continue to experience. A Pew Research Center survey released in October 2017 showed that such obstacles exist throughout most US industries. One example that Pew singled out is the tech industry, involving computers, all sorts of digital software, and information industries in general. The study found that fully 73 percent of Americans—women and men alike—viewed discrimination against women in the tech industry as a definite issue. Moreover, 37 percent said it was a major problem.

Interestingly, women's ages play a role in how they see that problem. Forty-nine percent, or about half, of women younger than fifty said gender discrimination occurs in that industry. In comparison, only 37 percent of women over fifty said that. The reasons for this disparity remain unclear. But some experts think that it is because older

> "[Some] employers maintain policies that punish employees who voluntarily share salary information with their coworkers."[58]
>
> —National Women's Law Center

women grew up when gender biases were more widespread and over time have grown used to them.

The Pew Research Center adds that these figures for gender discrimination in the tech industry closely mirror those in society's workplaces as a whole. In 2014, for instance, Pew found that 65 percent of American women said they had either experienced or witnessed such discrimination in the workplace. The 2014 and 2017 surveys also noted that prejudice against females in the workplace was even worse for black and Hispanic women.

Disparity between women's and men's wages is, of course, one of the more glaring of these prejudices, the studies showed. But there are others. According to Pew researchers Kim Parker and Cary Funk,

> Women are roughly four times as likely as men to say they have been treated as if they were not competent because of their gender (23% of employed women versus 6% of men), and they are about three times as likely as men to say they have experienced repeated small slights at work because of their gender (16% versus 5%). There are significant gaps on other items as well. While 15% of working women say they have received less support from senior leaders than a man who was doing the same job, only 7% of working men report having a similar experience. [Ten percent of] working women say they have been passed over for the most important assignments because of their gender, compared with 5% of men.[59]

A Reckoning Centuries in the Making

The fact that women have not yet achieved full equality with men—both inside and outside the workplace—has been clearly demonstrated by a social phenomenon that rocked the country during the second half of 2017. It bore several nicknames, but the most familiar was the #MeToo movement. It had been no secret to anyone that some men have sexually harassed women in various ways since time began. But not until mid-2017 did the enormous extent of the problem become clear.

The story began to break when movie producer Harvey Weinstein was accused by several women of harassing them in the past. Within mere weeks he had resigned from his own company, and dozens, and eventually hundreds, of other prominent men were also singled out by women as harassers. They included former Fox News host Bill O'Reilly, Minnesota senator Al Franken, and hip-hop mogul Russell Simmons. In addition, more than a dozen women who had accused President Donald Trump of the same thing back in 2016 came forward and repeated their claims.

On witnessing this virtual tsunami of accusations, many people thought back to the 1991 senatorial hearings to approve Judge Clarence Thomas for a place on the US Supreme Court. During those hearings news headlines centered on a University of Oklahoma law professor named Anita Hill. She accused Thomas of repeatedly sexually harassing her when she had worked for him a few years before. Thomas denied the charge, and neither party could prove the other was lying. So the Senate confirmed him by a vote of fifty-two to forty-eight. Numerous Americans assumed that Hill had lied. But in the wake of the 2017 #MeToo movement, many of their number have come to believe her.

Furthermore, *Time* magazine chose as its 2017 Person of the Year the collective army of women who had stepped forward to see justice done. *Time*'s Stephanie Zacharek states,

This reckoning appears to have sprung up overnight. But it has actually been simmering for years, decades, centuries. Women have had it with bosses and co-workers who not only cross boundaries but don't even seem to know that boundaries exist. They've had it with the fear of retaliation, of being blackballed, of being fired from a job they can't afford to lose. They've had it with the code of going along to get along. They've had it with men who use their power to take what they want from women. These silence breakers have started a revolution of refusal, gathering strength by the day.[60]

Zacharek's assertion that the emotions fueling the #MeToo movement had been building up well before mid-2017 was well illustrated by the enormous demonstrations that took place in towns and cities across the country on January 21, 2017. It was the largest single-day protest in US history. Collectively called "the Women's March," these nationwide rallies were character-

In January 2018 many thousands of women and men marched in Los Angeles and other cities across the United States to protest against policies of President Donald Trump that threaten to eliminate hard-fought gains by women.

ized by protests over the newly elected US president and his statements and policies concerning women, immigrants, the environment, and more. Carrying on the tradition begun the year before, on January 20, 2018, hundreds of thousands of protesters again took to the streets in cities and towns all across America for the second Women's March. Many marchers focused on the same issues as the year before, but this time they also highlighted concerns about sexual harassment and encouraged women to vote and run for office.

> "This revolution is too just, too important, and too long overdue."[61]
>
> —Leading feminist Gertrude Mongella

Time, Strength, and Moral Ammunition

The ultimate outcome of such marches and the #MeToo movement and how they will impact the larger, ongoing feminist movement as a whole remain unknown. More certain is that the cultural revolution that the women's rights movement has been effecting for more than a century will go on, almost certainly until it attains all its goals. "There is no going back," asserts leading feminist Gertrude Mongella. "This revolution is too just, too important, and too long overdue."[61]

In looking toward the future, as Mongella insists is essential, some women have reached back and embraced a sliver of wisdom from the past. Back in 1848, in addressing those who had gathered for the very first women's rights convention, Elizabeth Cady Stanton delivered a few stirring sentences that remain, and perhaps always will remain, a creed for all women who strive for equality. "It is our duty," she stated, "to assert and reassert this right to [protest], discuss, and petition, until our political equality be fully recognized." Women must attack the "fortress" of traditional male domination, she said. "Let us encamp right under its shadow," she continued, and "there spend all our time, strength, and moral ammunition, year after year, with perseverance, courage, and decision."[62]

SOURCE NOTES

Introduction: American Suffragists and the Night of Terror

1. Quoted in Women in History Ohio, "Alice Paul." www.women inhistoryohio.com.
2. Quoted in Women in History Ohio, "Alice Paul."
3. Quoted in Women in History Ohio, "Alice Paul."
4. Quoted in Inez H. Gillmore, *The Story of the Woman's Party*. New York: Harcourt, Brace, 1921, p. 274.
5. Terence McArdle, "'Night of Terror': The Suffragists Who Were Beaten and Tortured for Seeking the Vote," *Washington Post*, November 10, 2017. www.washingtonpost.com.
6. Alice Paul Institute, "Who Was Alice Paul?" www.alicepaul.org.

Chapter One: Centuries of Second-Class Citizenship

7. Quoted in Institute for Intercultural Studies, "Frequently Asked Questions About Mead/Bateson." www.interculturalstudies.org.
8. Bonnie Eisenberg and Mary Ruthsdotter, "History of the Women's Rights Movement," National Women's History Project. www.nwhp.org.
9. Quoted in J.K. Hosner, ed., *John Winthrop's Journal, 1630–1649*, vol. 2. New York: Scribner's, 1908, p. 239.
10. Catherine A. Brekus, "Women and Religion in Colonial North America and the United States," *Oxford Research Encyclopedia of American History*, May 2017. http://americanhistory.oxfordre.com.
11. Elizabeth G. Speare, *Life in Colonial America*. New York: Random House, 1963, p. 69.
12. Anne Bradstreet, "Four Ages of Man," Early Americas Digital Library. http://eada.lib.umd.edu.
13. Hannah Mather Crocker, *Observations on the Real Rights of Women*. Boston: printed by the author, 1818, p. 41. https://books.google.com.
14. Faye E. Dudden, "Women's Rights, Abolitionism, and Reform in Antebellum and Gilded Age America," *Oxford Research Encyclopedia of American History*, April 2016. http://americanhistory.oxfordre.com.

15. Quoted in Elizabeth Cady Stanton, Susan B. Anthony, and Matilda Joslyn Gage, eds., *History of Woman Suffrage*, vol. 1. New York: Fowler & Wells, 1881, p. 67.
16. Elizabeth Cady Stanton, "Address by Elizabeth Cady Stanton on Woman's Rights, September 1848," Elizabeth Cady Stanton and Susan B. Anthony Papers Project. http://ecssba.rutgers.edu.
17. Quoted in Constance B. Rynder, "Seneca Falls Convention," HistoryNet. www.historynet.com.

Chapter Two: Women Learn to Fight for Their Rights

18. Quoted in AwesomeStories, "Suffragists: Heroes of the Civil Rights Movement." www.awesomestories.com.
19. Quoted in AwesomeStories, "Declaration of Sentiments—No—Mechanic's Advocate." www.awesomestories.com.
20. Eisenberg and Ruthsdotter, "History of the Women's Rights Movement."
21. Quoted in Brenda Stalcup, ed., *Opposing Viewpoints: The Women's Rights Movement*. San Diego: Greenhaven, 1996, p. 85.
22. Quoted in Joel Myerson et al., eds., *The Journals of Louisa May Alcott*. Athens: University of Georgia Press, 1997, p. 27.
23. James Dunn, "The Angel of the Battlefield," in *Clara Barton Papers*, Library of Congress, Washington, DC.
24. Quoted in Barbara M. Wertheimer, *We Were There: The Story of Working Women in America*. New York: Pantheon, 1997, p. 143.
25. Quoted in Eleanor Flexner and Ellen Fitzpatrick, *Century of Struggle: The Women's Rights Movement in the United States*. Cambridge, MA: Harvard University Press, 1996, p. 138.
26. Quoted in Elizabeth Frost and Kathryn Cullen-Dupont, eds., *Women's Suffrage in America: An Eyewitness History*. New York: Facts On File, 2005, p. 202.
27. Elizabeth Gurley Flynn, "Women in Industry Should Organize," in *Words on Fire: The Life and Writing of Elizabeth Gurley Flynn*, ed. Rosalyn Fraad Baxandall. New Brunswick, NJ: Rutgers University Press, 1987, p. 96.
28. *New York Times*, "141 Men and Girls Die in Waist Factory Fire; Trapped High Up in Washington Place Building Street Strewn with Bodies; Piles of Dead Inside," March 26, 1911, NYTimes.com.

29. Kathleen M. Blee, "Antifeminism," in *The Reader's Companion to U.S. Women's History*, ed. Wilma Mankiller et al. Boston: Houghton Mifflin, 1999, p. 32.
30. Quoted in Sara H. Graham, *Women Suffrage and the New Democracy*. New Haven, CT: Yale University Press, 1996, p. 106.
31. Quoted in Robert P.J. Cooney Jr., *Winning the Vote: The Triumph of the American Woman Suffrage Movement*. Santa Cruz, CA: American Graphic, 2005, p. 437.
32. Quoted in Cooney, *Winning the Vote*, p. 437.

Chapter Three: Battles for Recognition and Jobs
33. Emily Spivack, "The History of the Flapper, Part 1: A Call to Freedom," *Smithsonian*, February 5, 2013. www.smithsonian mag.com.
34. Quoted in Spivack, "The History of the Flapper, Part 1."
35. Sara M. Evans, *Born for Liberty: A History of Women in America*. New York: Free Press, 1997, p. 185.
36. Quoted in Steven Mintz and Sara McNeill, "Great Depression and the New Deal," Digital History, 2016. www.digitalhistory .uh.edu.
37. Elaine T. May, "Pushing the Limits, 1940–1961," in *No Small Courage: A History of Women in the United States*, ed. Nancy F. Cott. New York: Oxford University Press, 2000, p. 491.
38. Evans, *Born for Liberty*, p. 253.
39. Quoted in Judith Hole and Ellen Levine, *Rebirth of Feminism*. New York: Quadrangle, 1971, p. 84.
40. Estelle B. Freedman, *No Turning Back: The History of Feminism and the Future of Women*. New York: Ballantine, 2002, p. 176.

Chapter Four: Striving for True Equality
41. Quoted in Jane J. Manbridge, *Why We Lost the ERA*. Chicago: University of Chicago Press, 1986, p. 104.
42. Quoted in National Woman's Party, "Women's History in the U.S." http://nationalwomansparty.org.
43. Linda Napikoski, "Gloria Steinem: Feminist and Editor," ThoughtCo, March 18, 2017. www.thoughtco.com.
44. Quoted in Eisenberg and Ruthsdotter, "History of the Women's Movement."

45. Quoted in Nancy MacLean, ed., *The American Women's Movement, 1945–2000*. New York: St. Martin's, 2009, p. 114.
46. USHistory.org, "*Roe v. Wade* and Its Impact." www.ushistory .org.
47. Flexner and Fitzpatrick, *Century of Struggle*, p. 327.
48. MacLean, *The American Women's Movement, 1945–2000*, p. 41.
49. Matthew Wasniewski, "The Year of the Woman, 1992," History, Art & Archives, US House of Representatives, Office of the Historian. http://history.house.gov.
50. Matthew Wasniewski, "Forging Lasting Institutional Change," History, Art & Archives, US House of Representatives, Office of the Historian. http://history.house.gov.
51. Lindy West, "Her Loss," Voices4Hillary. www.voices4hillary .com.

Chapter Five: The Struggle for Equality Goes On
52. Freedman, *No Turning Back*, p. 345.
53. Freedman, *No Turning Back*, p. 346.
54. MacLean, *The American Women's Movement, 1945–2000*, p. 38.
55. Quoted in *New York Times*, "Woman Cadet Graduates at the Citadel, a First," May 9, 1999. www.nytimes.com.
56. Quoted in CBS News, "Current and Former Cadets Speak Out on Sexual Assault at Air Force Academy," December 12, 2017. www.cbsnews.com.
57. National Women's Law Center, "The Lilly Ledbetter Act Five Years Later—a Law That Works." https://nwlc.org.
58. National Women's Law Center, "The Lilly Ledbetter Act Five Years Later."
59. Kim Parker and Cary Funk, "Gender Discrimination Comes in Many Forms for Today's Working Women," Pew Research Center, December 14, 2017. www.pewresearch.org.
60. Stephanie Zacharek, Eliana Dockterman, and Haley Sweetland Edwards, "The Silence Breakers," *Time*, December 18, 2017. http://time.com.
61. Gertrude Mongella, "Moving Beyond Rhetoric," in *Women Looking Backward*, edited by the United Nations. New York: United Nations, 2000, p. 121.
62. Quoted in National Woman's Party, "Women's History in the U.S."

FOR FURTHER RESEARCH

Books

Lara Antal, *The Women's Suffrage Movement*. New York: Cavendish Square, 2017.

Kathryn J. Atwood, *Women Heroes of World War II: 26 Stories of Espionage, Sabotage, Resistance, and Rescue*. Chicago: Chicago Review, 2013.

Nadia A. Higgins, *Feminism: Reinventing the F-Word*. Minneapolis: Twenty-First Century, 2016.

Kelly Jensen, *Here We Are: Feminism for the Real World*. New York: Algonquin Young Readers, 2017.

Deborah Kent, *The Seneca Falls Convention: Working to Expand Women's Rights*. Berkeley Heights, NJ: Enslow, 2016.

Laura B. Litwin, *Susan B. Anthony: Social Reformer and Feminist*. Berkeley Heights, NJ: Enslow, 2016.

Julie Murphy and Sandhya Menon, *Our Stories, Our Voices: 21 YA Authors Get Real About Injustice, Empowerment, and Growing Up Female in America*. New York: Simon Pulse, 2018.

Internet Sources

Alice Paul Institute, "Who Was Alice Paul?" www.alicepaul.org /who-was-alice-paul.

Bonnie Eisenberg and Mary Ruthsdotter, "History of the Women's Rights Movement," National Women's History Project. www .nwhp.org/resources/womens-rights-movement/history-of-the -womens-rights-movement.

Kate Pickert, "Lilly Ledbetter," *Time*, January 29, 2009. http:// content.time.com/time/nation/article/0,8599,1874954,00.html.

Emily Spivack, "The History of the Flapper, Part 1: A Call to Freedom," *Smithsonian*, February 5, 2013. www.smithsonianmag. com/arts-culture/the-history-of-the-flapper-part-1-a-call-for-free dom-11957978.

74

Elizabeth Cady Stanton, "Address by Elizabeth Cady Stanton on Woman's Rights, September 1848," Elizabeth Cady Stanton and Susan B. Anthony Papers Project. http://ecssba.rutgers.edu/docs/ecswoman1.html.

Mary Wang, "Gloria Steinem's Advice for the Next Generation of Feminists Is a Must-Read for Our Time," *Vogue*, October 13, 2017. www.vogue.com/article/Gloria-steinem-robin-morgan-festival-albertine-feminist-next-generation.

Websites

National Woman's Party (http://nationalwomansparty.org). This useful website offers not only a brief history of women's efforts to gain civil rights in the United States but also links to other related issues.

National Women's History Project (www.nwhp.org/). This site provides information on the historic accomplishments of women. It includes links to a history and timeline of the women's rights movement, articles describing how women won the right to vote, and other topics of interest.

"The Women's Rights Movement, 1848–1920." (http://history.house.gov/Exhibitions-and-Publications/WIC/Historical-Essays/No-Lady/Womens-Rights/). This thoughtful, informative site provided by Matthew Wasniewski, the historian of the US House of Representatives, has articles and links to many topics related to women's rights, plus detailed biographies of the various women who have served in Congress.

INDEX

Note: Boldface page numbers indicate illustrations.

wage discrimination, 62–65

Washington Post (newspaper), 9

Wasniewski, Matthew, 52, 54–55

Weinstein, Harvey, 67

West, Lindy, 57

West Point, US Military Academy at, 61

Whittaker, W.H., 7, 8–9

Willard, Emma, 16

Wilson, Woodrow, 6–7, 9, 32–33

Winthrop, John, 11

women
in Civil War, 24–26, **25**
gain voting rights, 32–33
in government/politics, 34, 39–40, 54–57
in Jazz Age, 34–38, **35**
in military, 40–41, **59,** 59—62
1950s' ideal of, 42–43
status in early America, 11–15
wage discrimination against, 62–65

workplace discrimination against, 65–66
in World War II, 40–41

"Women in Industry Should Organize" (Flynn), 30

Women's March, 67–68, **68**

women's rights movement
beginnings of, 10
important events in, **4–5**
1960s resurgence of, 44–45

"The Women's Rights Movement, 1848–1920" (website), 75

Woodward, Charlotte, 22

workforce, women in
discrimination against, 62–66
in early America, 16–17, **17**
fight to improve working conditions and, 27–30, **29**
increase of, 43–44
during World War II, 40

Wright, Frances, 16, 18

Year of the Woman (1992), 54–55